Man May Condemn, *but* **God** Gives Grace

By: Brianna Echavarria

Copyright Page Man Condemns, but God Gives Grace

Copyright © 2026 by Brianna Echavarria

All rights reserved. No part of this book may be reproduced, stored in a retrieval system, or transmitted in any form or by any means without prior written permission from the author, except for brief quotations in reviews or articles.

Scripture quotations are taken from the Holy Bible, New International Version® (NIV). Used by permission.

Printed in the United States of America.

ISBN 979-8-218-93864-2

Dedication

For Noel, Nathan, and Noah.

You are my heart, my joy, and my why.

## Table of Contents

Opening: Thank you, Jesus! — Pg. 5

Chapter 1: God's Grace and Wisdom — Pg. 7

Chapter 2: My Darkness Will Be Your Light — Pg. 16

Chapter 3: Keep Going — Pg. 26

Chapter 4: Strange Grace — Pg. 31

Chapter 5: We Still Made It — Pg. 37

Chapter 6: Heal — Pg. 44

Chapter 7: Surprise — Pg. 52

A Friendly 7-Day Identity Devotional — Pg. 59

Closing: Dear Readers, Prayer — Pg. 68

**Opening:** Thank You, Jesus!

## *Psalms 9: 1-2 (NIV)*

*I will give thanks to you, Lord, with all my heart; I will tell of all your wonderful deeds. (2) I will be glad and rejoice in you; I will sing the praises of your name, O Most High.*

Who would have imagined that I'd find myself writing this book? Well, Jesus did, and let me tell you—His protection, guidance, and love have been breathtaking. I must begin by expressing my deepest gratitude: thank you, Jesus. Thank you for seeing potential in me when I couldn't see it within myself. Thank you for entrusting me with the purpose you have in mind and for believing in me, especially during times when I struggled to believe in myself.

We often think we have complete control over our lives, but the truth is quite different. None of us is truly self-made, no matter how much we might claim it; we are all Jesus-made. I invite you on this journey with me—are you prepared to receive the incredible blessings God has in store for you? This journey requires us to surrender our plans and the illusion of control.

To my husband, Noel, and my sons, Nathan and Noah. Each day, I pray for your protection and hope you will find pride in me and my work. While the world may have mixed feelings about what I create, your love and support mean everything to me.

I identify as an underdog, and while that might feel daunting, I carry with me the certainty that I will always prevail because I never fight alone. The outcomes of my battles may not always align with my expectations, but they are ultimately what God has designed for me. Even when my plans leave scars, I trust that Jesus will transform them into something beautiful.

This book will take you on an emotional rollercoaster, but remember, my story and your story aren't finished until we see the Lord face-to-face. Embrace this healing journey with me; we will witness how faith can illuminate our lives together. I pray that as you read these words, you are enveloped by the Lord's love and feel His presence surrounding you, offering comfort and strength.

## Chapter 1: God's Grace and Wisdom

### *Psalms 139:16-18 (NIV)*

*Your eyes saw my unformed body; all the days ordained for me were written in your book before one of them came to be. (17) How precious to me are your thoughts, God. How vast is the sum of them! (18) Where I to count them, they would outnumber the grains of sand- when I awake, I am still with you.*

As an adult, a mom, a wife, and a woman, I often question my worth, wondering if I am good enough, loved enough, or smart enough. I want to share that even as I write this book, I attend therapy weekly, allowing myself the space to process everything I'm working through. My childhood experiences and struggles with reading have left me grappling with the echoes of words spoken over me. It's a common misconception that with age, the pain disappears. In truth, just because time passes doesn't mean the wounds heal completely; they can resurface unexpectedly. Regardless of my accomplishments, praise from others, or how incredible I am perceived, I continue to doubt my self-worth because a thought can turn into a feeling faster than you can blink. I want to emphasize that healing is a journey, and it's perfectly acceptable to seek support before we proceed further.

I want to share something deeply personal about how God brought this book to me. It all started with an assignment in my doctoral program, the first class and assignment in my Ed.D. journey. We were asked to reflect on our "aha" moments that makes you want to go into higher education, and it truly sparked something within me. Reflecting on my journey to learn to read and ultimately graduate high school, I realize that while I often celebrated finishing in four years despite significant challenges, I had never truly taken the time to process the hardships along the way.

In a matter of minutes, while outlining this paper for class, I was hit with the reminder of feeling overwhelmed in a crowded classroom, struggling with phonics while my peers seemed to excel, being called every name in the book, but a child of God, and more. Every challenge, including multiple reading classes at school, late nights of studying, and the steadfast support from my teachers and family, played an essential role in my journey. Yet, for some reason, my mind has relegated these memories to a different universe within my brain until I had to complete this assignment.

Writing about my journey brought forth a flood of emotions. I cried for three days as I outlined the challenges I faced. I turned to my husband and therapist, seeking comfort and understanding. I went to seek their help when the Lord should have been the first person, I sought comfort and understanding from. I made calls to my grandma and my nanna to gather their insights, which unintentionally resurfaced old feelings of anger related to my experiences with reading and the lack of support I had encountered. It was deeply upsetting to reveal their emotions of hurt and disappointment with the school system and their anger towards the resistance faced while advocating for me, especially given how long they had suppressed these feelings.

During my conversations with my grandmother and my nanna, they often expressed their discomfort, saying, "Ugh, I really don't want to talk about this right now, or

I'm just going to get upset all over again." Their words resonated with me deeply. My grandma even shared a story about how, while in Union Middle School, she wrote a letter to the school expressing her concerns about my learning difficulties. She explained that she had to visit the school because they were not taking her letter seriously. Unfortunately, she discovered that we had missed the deadline for me to be tested. However, the principal worked with my grandmother and insisted that the teachers do whatever was necessary to provide me with the extra help I needed.

    I could feel the weight of their emotions and the memories that tied them to this painful subject. While I found myself eager to revisit and process this particular wound, I also strongly wanted to honor their feelings and respect their boundaries. It became clear that just because I was ready to confront the past didn't mean they were in the same place. Their hesitations were a reminder that healing is a personal journey, and we each have our timeline for tackling such difficult issues.

    Now, I understand that revisiting certain experiences can reopen wounds that haven't fully healed, both from childhood and into adulthood. It's important to recognize that just as physical wounds can become infected and lead to serious illness, emotional wounds can also profoundly impact our well-being. Lately, I feel the need to peel back the layers I've built over these emotional injuries because if I don't, I risk being consumed by bitterness, rage, and anger, which could hinder me from achieving my true calling and purpose in life.

    It's natural to have scars; they are part of our story. However, we must be cautious of wounds, which can be destructive if left unaddressed. I've been praying for the strength to soften my heart and to reveal the hidden wounds that need healing. I'm ready and eager to embrace my battle scars, knowing they reflect my journey and resilience. I understand that some might not relate to me or may even dismiss my feelings, but these scars represent overcoming challenges and emerging stronger than before. Conversely, wounds can leave us feeling broken, sad, and bitter, and it's crucial to face them to find healing.

    God gave me my greatest gift through my most challenging moment: the gift of advocacy, the pen to write, my voice to speak up for others, and the determination that supersedes anyone and any situation. Initially, I found myself reflecting on my journey as a victim, feeling the weight of all my struggles, the laughter directed at me, and the negative words spoken over me. I began to relive the hurt and pain I had yet to process, let alone heal from. Then, I reminded myself to guard my mind, as thoughts of worthlessness crept in. Despite holding a high school diploma, a bachelor's degree, and a Master's degree—and currently pursuing an Ed.D.—I often find myself questioning my worth. I am married to an incredible man who supports me wholeheartedly, and I am blessed with two beautiful boys. Yet, as I embark on the journey of writing a book, something entirely new to me and both thrilling and daunting, I can't shake this nagging feeling of inadequacy. I had to remind myself every day it wasn't God speaking to me; it was the enemy trying to exploit my moment of weakness. We must examine what we think about and ask ourselves if these thoughts reflect the way the Lord, who created me, sees me.

**To this day**, I need to remind myself of the identity the Lord says I possess. Let me share a current story from my life that illustrates this struggle. My first son is three, but when he was just a year old, I embraced the role of a stay-at-home mom, dedicating my days to nurturing him. During that time, I read to him daily, immersing myself in the pages of storybooks. Each night, my husband and I would take turns reading the Bible together, creating a sacred routine we cherished as a family.

While we were engrossed in our reading one evening, we had a close family member on the phone. In an unexpected moment, they criticized how I was reading, saying, "Why are you reading like that? You sound terrible. He will not learn to read the way you're reading. Noel, please take over and read the book to Nathan." Their words stung like a sharp arrow, piercing through the warmth of our family bonding. I tried to laugh it off, brushing aside the comment and assuring that person we would call them the next day since it was getting late and Nathan needed to get to bed. But that night, as I stepped into the shower, the weight of their words sank in, and I cried quietly.

From that moment, I gravitated away from reading to my son. For six long months, I created a smokescreen of excuses to avoid our nightly Bible readings. I convinced myself it would be a special father-son bonding moment, all while it was really a reflection of my deep-seated fear—fear that I would somehow harm my child's learning because I struggle with reading. Though I could read fluently in my mind and comprehend everything perfectly, when it came to vocalizing the words out loud, my dyslexia became glaringly apparent. The thought of reading aloud filled me with anxiety, as I dreaded the possibility of being laughed at or ridiculed again.

Unbeknownst to me, I had allowed this stronghold of fear to dictate my actions and silence my voice for far too long. My husband remained oblivious to my struggle, unaware of the real reason behind my absence from Storytime. When he finally reads this chapter, it will be the first inkling he has of my internal battle. The turning point came when my husband was deployed for six months. The thought of our son falling asleep without his cherished Bible stories tugged at my heart. I realized I couldn't let fear continue to hold me and prevent my son from hearing the amazing stories about Jesus. God needed to remind me of my worth and that I could still be a source of love and knowledge for my son despite the laughter, judgment, or belittlement from others. That sacred time returned to our routine and, with it, a renewed sense of purpose.

God is not only creative but also the Creator. He created me in the image He needed and desired for His kingdom. God can transform nothing into everything and utilize the most unlikely people to convey His messages. The real question is whether we are willing to be used, even though we are in trials. God entrusted me to revisit and relive a moment my mind deliberately tried to forget. Sometimes, I ponder whether our most significant challenges are not crashes but callings from God. He didn't promise us life would be perfectly easy with no trials, but He did assure us of His presence. I once thought my struggles—being unable to read, being labeled as dumb, being bullied, and being told I would become a stripper—were my destiny. These were not part of my destiny, nor have they ever been part of it, but they are part of my calling by leading me to share my story with you today.

## Journal Reflection Prompt

*Reflect on an event or challenge from your past that continues to cast a shadow over your life today. What is this lingering experience that still holds a strong grip on you, shaping your thoughts and actions?*

**Jeremiah 30:17 (NIV)**

*"But I will restore you to health and heal your wounds."*

**Chapter 2:** My Darkness Will Be Your Light

### *Psalms 9: 13-14 (NIV)*

*Lord, see how my enemies persecute me! Have mercy and lift me up from the gates of death, (14) that I may declare your praises in the gates of Daughter Zion, and there rejoice in your salvation.*

---

Reflecting on my childhood, where it all began, I recall how teachers in elementary and middle school labeled me "bad." Yet, my grandma and nanna recognized my learning, reading, and writing struggles, which showed as behavior issues. They fought tirelessly to ensure I received the help needed to succeed, but obstacles often hindered their efforts. They were writing letters to the board of education, reaching out to my teachers, and speaking with the principal. Although my memories from that time are hazy, I vividly remember how their unwavering support laid the foundation for my future. Their belief in my potential instilled hope that propelled me forward. It serves as a reminder that even in our darkest moments, someone can shine a light and guide us toward a better path. Their impact taught me the value of perseverance and the importance of seeking help. No matter how challenging the journey may seem, we can rise above and achieve our dreams with the proper support.

Two days before I was scheduled to attend my hometown high school, my name was picked out of a lottery for a charter school in another city. On short notice, I was expected to start high school at a new school in a new town with no friends. I was an outsider from day one. My very first class was English, and the teacher asked each person to read a sentence from a book in front of the class. When my turn came, I could not read one word without the teacher telling me what the word was. The teacher didn't think much of it until my turn came around again. I still couldn't read one word without her assistance. The class laughed at me, and one kid yelled, "She can't read! She is retarded." Back then, when I was in high school retarded was a normal word and not looked down on. My teacher never reprimanded the student, and I was humiliated. Rather than addressing the student, she casually continued her lesson and stopped the class from participating in the reading-aloud activity. This was one day of several years of high school bullying to follow.

      That afternoon, my parents received a call from the school asking them to come in at the end of the day to pick me up and meet with the guidance counselor. In the cozy yet professional office filled with books and posters about emotional well-being, the counselor explained the incident that transpired in my English class. They expressed their concerns about my struggles with reading and comprehension and suggested that I might benefit from being tested for a learning disability. Before proceeding with the testing, they required my parents' consent to sign some paperwork.

      After a brief discussion, my parents agreed to the testing, hoping to get to the root of my difficulties. The assessment process spanned an entire week and was packed with multiple sessions that felt like a marathon. Each day, I was escorted into a testing room, equipped with a table covered in sheets of paper and colorful yet intimidating flashcards. As I tackled various tasks—from memory exercises that involved recalling sequences of numbers and words to reading passages aloud and answering comprehension questions, I often felt a growing sense of unease. Each time I stumbled over a word or couldn't remember details, it chipped away at my self-esteem, leaving me feeling increasingly inadequate. The cumulative effect of those sessions left me drained, burdened with a sense of helplessness and defeat that weighed heavily on my heart by the time I exited the room each day.

My parents were called into a meeting with the principal, my guidance counselor, and the administrator who tested me. The administrator explained the results of my tests. I couldn't understand what was being said, the questions being asked, or the plans they were creating for me. Eventually, the administrator said,

> "Brianna, I know you may not understand all of this, but I want you to know you are in the 9th grade, but on a 3rd-grade reading level. You can't read or comprehend anything. You have a learning disability of reading comprehension, and you are also dyslexic. You will, therefore, not graduate from high school in four years with your peers. You will be here for six to seven years, and college will not be an option."

All I remember saying was, "Okay."

The new plan involved me attending three different English classes every day with roughly five other students. That same day, one of my close family members started calling me "dumb," "stupid," and "a disappointment." Another family member said, "I was lucky I knew how to dance, and I was pretty because that was the only way I was going to make it in life."

I was navigating a world filled with

misunderstanding, confusion, and challenges. Though I felt the weight of misunderstanding and mistreatment, I now recognize those struggles as part of my journey. At 14, I faced discouragement and harsh words that suggested I would be nothing, yet those experiences have fueled my determination. While opportunities seemed denied before they even reached me, I've come to understand that I have the power to create my path. By the time I reached 11$^{th}$ grade, I had progressed significantly. I started reading at a 10th-grade reading level. The first book I could read on my own was *The Hunger Games*. Hold on to your seats because we are about to see just how God's Grace is about to take over and work in the life of a 14-year-old black girl living in the inner city of Newark, NJ.

Another meeting was held to discuss my improvements. The administrators suggested that I take the HESPA test, but not to get our hopes up about my passing. I remember running to the bathroom to cry. Sharmine Bolden, one of my teachers, cheerleading coach, and mentor, assured me, "Not only will I take the test, but I will pass it with flying colors". I remember laughing like it was the funniest thing I've ever heard. I responded: "Were you not in the same meeting as me"? Ms. Bolden said, "They are also the same ones who said you would never catch up to your grade reading level, and you did. Just as you have been proving them wrong, you will keep proving them wrong."

**She was right!** I scored proficiently in reading and writing, and highly proficient in Math. I was well on my way to graduating in four years! By senior year, I took one English class with my 12th-grade peers. Additionally, I was inducted into the National Honor Society. I started applying for college, and I wanted to apply to as many as possible because I didn't know which ones I would be able to get into.

During my last high school Individualized Education Program (IEP) meeting, my advisors emphasized my potential challenges in college. For the first time, I advocated for myself and told them, "I am tired of you all telling me what I can and cannot do. I will apply to college, and I will graduate from college," and walked out of that room. It was a humbling acknowledgment that, by God's grace, I had increased my reading skills by an astonishing nine grade levels in just three years. What else was possible if God could accomplish such a remarkable transformation in my life?

Every Sunday morning, without fail, my church family made it a point for me to read aloud during Sunday school and morning service. No matter how long it took, my church family was always there, patiently guiding me through the words during service time. Mr. Dockins, one of my special education teachers, didn't just work with me during class; he would invite me into the classroom at lunchtime, where we would share meals while diving into a world full of stories. He even devised engaging games that turned spelling and writing into fun challenges on the whiteboard, transforming my learning experience.

Ms. Silberstein was another unwavering anchor in my educational journey. She made sure I stayed laser-focused during our intimate special education reading classes. There were days when I felt like throwing in the towel, feeling overwhelmed and defeated, but she would never allow me to succumb to those doubts. She kept distractions at bay with a steadfast determination and always encouraged me to rise above my struggles, making sure I didn't wallow in self-pity.

After cheerleading practice, Ms. Bolden, my coach, would often linger long after the other girls had gone home, dedicating her evenings to helping me improve my reading skills. She sacrificed her own time, frequently returning home late to her husband, all for my benefit. Her commitment didn't stop there; she pushed me in math, encouraging me to take on honors courses to ensure I excelled across all subjects. She never allowed my struggles in reading to overshadow my potential in any other area.

Out of all my teachers who poured their hearts and souls into me over those four challenging years, I know I gave Ms. Bolden the hardest time. Despite her frustration and annoyance, she never gave up on me. These three remarkable educators and my church family at the Community Church of God in Newark, NJ, stood by me steadfastly. I believe God orchestrated the perfect individuals to guide me, implementing the miracles I needed in my life at the right moment. Their unwavering faith and support transformed my journey, proving that no challenge is insurmountable with the right people by your side.

Take a moment to let that sink in—nine entire reading grade levels in only three years! Some might say that's impossible, but it is a testament that God works in ways we can't always understand or foresee. He has the power to do the unimaginable. So, when facing challenges or doubts, remember that incredible things can happen with faith. Keep believing, and never underestimate what God can do in your life!

Graduation was a very special moment for me. Thankfully, I graduated high school at the top of my class and was also accepted to 12 out of the 14 universities I applied to. I remember sitting on the graduation stage, thinking about accomplishing a degree I was told I would never get. I beat every oddball against me despite the lack of support from certain family members, the education system, certain teachers at my high school, and even some of my peers around me. I made it, and I needed to keep making it. I needed to learn about a world I was told would not be for me, experience what I was not worthy of, and be a part of a world I was told I was not smart enough for. Education became my saving grace, and I was determined to achieve more than a high school diploma. **I could not stop there!** Not only was I told I would never graduate or attend college when I finally reached the level of graduating high school, but no one prepared me for what was to come. I had to learn how to advocate for myself and look for resources, and I even missed out on resources during my first four years of college.

My journey has been anything but easy, but each challenge has paved the way for my resilience and determination. My bachelor's and master's degrees are more than just qualifications; they are symbols of defiance against those who doubted me. Despite the skepticism from the world, the educational system, and even those close to me, I found unwavering support in my grandmothers, my church family, and inspiring teachers and mentors like Ms. Bolden, Ms. Silberstein, and Mr. Dockins.

I want to take a moment to express my gratitude for all the special education teachers out there. Your dedication and selfless work often go unnoticed, but it truly makes a difference in the lives of your students. Thank you for being a guiding light and for the impact you have had, both past and present. You are changing lives in ways that may not always be recognized, but your efforts are deeply appreciated!

Surprisingly, the struggles I faced, including being bullied and judged during my struggle to read, have become the fuel for my fire. The condemnation I faced before I even had a chance to prove myself has motivated me to rise, to pursue my doctorate in education, and to dedicate my life to God's kingdom work.

It's time to transform my darkness into light, using my experiences of pain and misunderstanding to inspire others. My trials have shaped my purpose and are guiding me toward my destiny. I believe my journey can illuminate the path for others, reminding them that we can create a brighter future even in adversity. Together, let's turn our struggles into strength and make a meaningful impact in the world!

## Journal Reflection Prompt

*How would you define your greatest accomplishments, and what does a thriving life look like for you? Let's explore what success means in your journey!*

**Romans 5:1 (NIV)**

*"Therefore, since we have been justified through faith, we have peace with God through our Lord Jesus Christ."*

**Chapter 3:** Keep Going

## *Psalms 56: 8-9 (NIV)*

*Record my misery; list my tears on your scroll are they not in your record? (9) Then my enemies will turn back when I call for help. By this, I will know that God is for me.*

Throughout this book, I move between my high school years, the beginning of my college journey, and the woman I am today. When I look back, I see an eighteen-year-old freshman filled with doubt—about my abilities, my future, and even God. I remember the tears I cried at night, the harsh words that echoed in my mind, and the frustration I directed toward the Lord. Belief felt heavy, and expectations felt impossible.

But as I explored that pain, something profound became clear. Every hurdle, every moment of anguish, shaped me into the resilient woman I am today. I questioned why things had to be so hard, why support felt absent, and why I always seemed to be climbing uphill. Through therapy and honest reflection, I realized those challenges refined my character and strengthened my spirit.

I learned it's okay to feel angry when you're wrestling with inadequacy. Acknowledging those emotions was a crucial step in my healing. Slowly, I began to see where God had been working in my life—even in the silence.

So I encourage anyone in a similar place: embrace your journey, including the uncomfortable parts. These experiences are forging you into someone stronger with a story worth telling. Healing is a process. It's never too late to ask for forgiveness—from yourself, from God, and from the journey that brought you here. You are not defined by your hardships but by how you rise from them. Your story is still being written, and the best is yet to come. Keep moving forward; you are stronger than you know.

When I look back at my struggles with reading, I remember the laughter of others ringing in my ears. But one thing remained constant: my situation didn't improve; I did. I became like a rock—unyielding in the face of adversity.

Nothing anyone says can break me now. I experienced that kind of vulnerability early, and it shaped me into someone who refuses to crumble. The bullying and the extra effort I had to put in lit a fire inside me—a desire to stand firm and lift others up.

If I could survive those years between fourteen and eighteen, you can survive your own battles too. Keep pushing forward. You are not alone.

In moments of doubt, we must anchor ourselves in the truth of who God is and the sacrifice made at the cross. Our God transcends every challenge we face. As His children, we are attuned to His voice, and it's crucial that we listen. God is always near, offering comfort and strength. When He feels distant, it's often because we haven't opened our hearts to Him. Embracing His love can transform hardship into growth.

Life gives us plenty of reasons to worry, but much of our anxiety stems from our own thoughts. When I think back to my freshman year of college, I realize I had little to fear. God had already walked that campus. He had already placed the right people in my path. The challenges were waiting, yes—but so was His provision.

On my first welcome day, I couldn't see the bigger picture. I worried about whether I would succeed, not realizing God already knew the outcome. Now, I challenge myself—and you—to pause when worry creeps in. Ask yourself:

Is this fear because I feel abandoned, or is God already working everything out and simply asking me to trust Him?

It's natural to cry and feel the weight of our emotions. Those feelings are valid. But with every tear, trust that God will not waste your pain. Each moment contributes to your growth and eventual triumph. Embrace your feelings, lean into your challenges, and remember: you are never alone.

## Journal Reflection Prompt

*In reflecting on the challenge from the Chapter 1 journal, consider how often worry takes over instead of trusting God's control. Are you genuinely seeking His guidance, or relying on your own understanding and the opinions of others?*

*How does this awareness shift your perspective on your challenges?*

**1 Samuel 24: 10 (NIV)**

*"This day you have seen me with your own eyes how the Lord delivered you into my hands in the cave. Some urged me to kill you, but I spare you; I said, 'I will not lay my hand on my lord, because he is the lord anointed."*

**Chapter 4**: Strange Grace

*<u>1 Samuel 24: 12-13 (NIV)</u>*

*May the Lord judge between you and me. And may the Lord avenge the wrongs you have done to me, but my hand will not touch you. (13) As the old saying goes, 'From evildoers come evil deeds,' so my hand will not touch you.*

I used to wrestle with deep questions for the Lord: Where were You during my struggles? Why did you allow certain people to give up on me or treat me as if I were less than? Those questions felt especially heavy when I thought about my childhood—a time when I needed guidance and love the most, even though I thought I was grown.

But in the middle of my questioning, something shifted. I began to see that God's grace had been present all along, just not in the ways I expected. It was a strange grace—subtle, quiet, and easy to overlook if I wasn't paying attention. Had I not been in a season of intimacy with the Lord, I might have missed these precious acts of love entirely.

Looking back now, I can see how His grace was woven through my challenges. There were moments of kindness from unexpected places—a teacher who believed in me, a friend who stood by me, or a quiet whisper of encouragement in my heart. Each encounter was a reminder of God's unwavering love, urging me to keep going.

I learned that grace doesn't always look like rescue. Sometimes it comes wrapped in hardship, disguised as disruption, or delivered through people we never expected. Yet those moments were shaping me, strengthening me, and guiding me toward who I was becoming.

Today, when I reflect on those difficult seasons, I'm not filled with bitterness. I'm filled with gratitude. Those experiences shaped me, and God's grace—strange, profound, and beautifully mysterious—was instrumental in my journey. I once placed God in a box defined by my expectations, but He is infinitely more.

As I considered the different ways the Lord showed up for me, I felt led to share a few pivotal moments where His strange grace carried me.

**1. Changing Schools**

This was one of the clearest examples of grace I didn't recognize at the time. I was registered to attend Union High School in Union, New Jersey—the same district I'd been in for four years. Two days before school started, I learned my name had been drawn in a lottery to attend Newark Collegiate Academy in Newark, NJ.

At first, it felt like a curse. A new school. A new city. No friends. No familiarity.

But Union, although knowing my learning difficulties, still had not helped me improve. They pushed me through the system with the No Child Left Behind program. Newark Collegiate Academy, despite the bullying and the loneliness, was the place where someone reached out beyond my grandparents and said, "She needs support."

And, in a twist only God could orchestrate, it was also the school where I met the friend who is now my husband.

Grace doesn't always look gentle. Sometimes it looks like being uprooted.

## 2. Three Transformative Teachers

Another profound act of grace came through three teachers who poured themselves into my education. They were young, fresh out of college, and faced with the challenge of teaching a student who was defiant, frustrated, and hurting.

One of them is now my son's godmother and the principal of that same school. She often tells stories about how she had to stand her ground with me, mirroring my own stubbornness. But beneath my attitude, she saw potential I couldn't see in myself.

Mr. Dockins and Ms. Silberstein were exceptional special education teachers. They understood that each student learns differently and adapted their teaching to meet us where we were. They recognized my strengths and weaknesses and tailored their lessons to fit me as an individual. Ms. Bolden wasn't a special education teacher, but she was a force in my life. She kept my attitude in check, pushed me academically, and saw my talent in math long before I did. She knew what I needed before I did.

- Ms. Silberstein chose books that captured my imagination.

- Mr. Dockins knew I needed movement and often took our reading classes outside.

I don't know their personal beliefs, but I know this: God used them. They were vessels of grace—unexpected, imperfect, and exactly who I needed.

Their influence motivates me to pour into other students the way they poured into me. They made sure I never felt invisible. They made sure I never felt alone.

**A Word to You, My Friend**

If you feel abandoned or overlooked, take a moment to look back. Grace may have shown up in ways you didn't recognize at the time. God often works through people, places, and disruptions we never would have chosen.

You are not alone.

And there is always a greater purpose at work.

## Journal Reflection Prompt

*While reflecting on past events or situations, can you identify moments where God showed up with unexpected grace?*

_____
_____
_____
_____
_____
_____
_____
_____
_____
_____
_____
_____
_____
_____
_____
_____
_____
_____
_____
_____
_____
_____
_____
_____
_____
_____
_____
_____
_____

_____
_____
_____
_____
_____
_____

*Here are three ways this might manifest:*

*1. Unforeseen Opportunities: During a difficult situation, you might have found a surprising opportunity that seemed out of place at the time. It could have been a job offer when you felt lost or a chance reunion with an old friend that brought comfort when you needed it most. This grace could have been a way for God to remind you that there is always hope, even in despair.*

*2. Unexpected Connections: Sometimes, the people we meet in trying times can provide support and encouragement we never anticipated. Someone's kindness or wisdom might have come through when you felt alone. Recognizing these divine appointments as acts of grace can help you see how God orchestrated relationships for your benefit.*

*3. Lessons Learned: Looking back, you may realize that your challenges taught you valuable lessons that shaped your character and faith. What felt like a setback at the time could have been a means of growth that allowed you to develop resilience or empathy for others. This realization can profoundly acknowledge God's grace in your life's journey.*

**Chapter 5:** We Still Made It

## *Isaiah 41:10 (NIV)*

*So do not fear, for I am with you; do not be dismayed, for I am your God. I will strengthen you and help you; I will uphold you with my righteous right hand.*

This is one of the hardest chapters for me to write. I titled it "We Still Made It," but sometimes it feels more like "We Are Still Making It." Every journey we complete opens the door to another one, and the wounds we reflect on now often resurface in new seasons. So, I find myself wondering: Will we ever truly "make it," or will I only know I've made it when I see the Lord face-to-face?

Still, the Lord reminded me that it's time to move forward and share this part of my story.

Here we are, exploring how we made it. I have to rely on the truth that God will never lead me into something He cannot carry me through. I didn't say He would remove me from it—because that's what we often want. We want God to take away the struggle, erase the pain, and let us wake up whole. I've prayed those prayers too: "Lord, let me wake up thinking only positive things about myself. Let me read better. Let me forget the pain others caused me."

But the truth is, we must walk through our trials. That's how we earn our battle scars and victories. That's how we share the gospel and testify to God's goodness.

The outcome won't always match our expectations. In fact, our expectations often limit what we believe God can do. The ending may not look like what we imagined, but the truth remains: you persevered, and God can work through it.

When I reflect on this message, I picture myself sitting in my first car.

Stay with me—this metaphor works.

## The Car Metaphor

Starting high school felt like driving a brand-new car. Everything looked perfect. But as the bullying began and the assessments revealed my reading struggles, it felt like warning lights started flashing on the dashboard. You know that moment when every light comes on, but you keep driving anyway, pretending nothing is wrong?

That was me.

Then came the testing, and the verdict felt devastating.

"You will never succeed."

It was like the battery and transmission failed at the same time. My once-shiny car suddenly broke down on the side of the road, collecting tickets while I sat inside, hoping it would magically start again.

But I kept trying. Every day, I climbed into that car, even though it wouldn't move. I kept hoping something would change.

As my teenage years unfolded, anger crept in. I found myself tangled in lies, toxic relationships, and the belief that any attention—even negative attention—was better than being invisible. My car kept deteriorating. The doors loosened. The structure weakened. It mirrored my internal world.

Then came a moment of clarity:

I needed to return to my faith.

It's easier to run to God when you know Him as a child than when you're an adult who feels disconnected. But returning is always possible—no matter your age.

By senior year, I had found my way back to the Lord. I felt ready to take on the world. But I still remember the surreal feeling of sitting in the driver's seat of my "car," with nothing left but the pedals and the seat on the ground beneath me. I was ready to drive, but I couldn't move.

That's exactly how my final high school days felt—full of desire but weighed down by everything I had survived.

### Carrying the Past Into the Future

Even after graduating, I carried the weight of my mistakes. I saw the hurt in my parents' eyes. I lost friendships I once cherished. I poured myself into relationships that didn't nourish me. My soul felt stretched thin.

But even then, God was guiding me.

He helped me navigate my disability.

He helped me step into college.

He helped me find purpose in the pain.

You may struggle to turn your pain into purpose, but the Lord is right there with you. He still wants to use you for kingdom work.

I often defined myself by my disability—by the way others judged my reading, by the labels placed on me. But I'm learning to remind myself daily of how the Lord sees me.

He never asked me to define myself by my failures, my trauma, or my challenges. He asked me to define myself by the identity He gave me before I was even born.

From Limiting Beliefs to Purpose

I used to ask God, "Why me?"

Why the battles?

Why the heaviness?

Why the self-doubt that still lingers?

But now I ask, "God, how can You use me through this?"

One day, I was journaling, and the prompt asked me to identify limiting beliefs I held about myself. It was eye-opening. Those beliefs were lies. When I journaled what I could accomplish without them, one thing stood out:

**Writing a book.**

I didn't know what the book would be about. I didn't know how to start. I was even afraid to apply for jobs I wanted because of my writing insecurities. But a week after that journaling session, the Lord gave me a complete outline for this book.

He had been preparing me all along.

This journey taught me the importance of recognizing my problems, acknowledging the pain, finding solutions, and seeking support.

I didn't want to be bullied.

I didn't want to feel less than.

I didn't want to be condemned as a child.

But I'm turning that challenge into my loudest sermon.

I was **bitten**, but I am **not bitter**.

That is my greatest blessing.

Not my high school diploma.

Not my bachelor's degree.

Not my master's degree.

Not even the doctoral degree I'm pursuing.

My greatest blessing is that I refused to hold onto bitterness.

God wouldn't have entrusted me with more if I hadn't survived what I did. He wouldn't have given me my degrees, my husband, my sons, or the opportunity to write this book.

We often ask God for more, but are we truly handling what He has already given us?

We pray for blessings, but are we ready for the challenges that come with them?

## Journal Reflection Prompt

*What have you been praying for lately?*

*Can you identify the challenges that might accompany the blessings you're asking for?*

*How can you strengthen your readiness while you wait?*

_____
_____
_____
_____
_____
_____
_____
_____
_____
_____
_____
_____
_____
_____
_____
_____
_____
_____
_____
_____
_____
_____
_____
_____

***Ephesians 6:16 (NIV)***

*"In addition to all this, take up the shield of faith, with which you can extinguish all the flaming arrows of the evil one. "*

## Chapter 6: Heal

### *James 2:13 (NIV)*

*Because judgment without mercy will be shown to anyone who has not been merciful. Mercy triumphs over judgment.*

When most people hear the word heal, a wave of anxiety rises within them. Healing brings old memories to the surface—memories of hurt, betrayal, disappointment, or situations we thought we had buried. I used to feel that same fear deeply. I believed there was no way I could forgive the people who had wronged me, whether individuals or institutions like the school system. It felt impossible, and that sense of helplessness echoed loudly in my thoughts.

But over time, something shifted. I realized that I, too, had caused pain in others' lives. I, too, longed for forgiveness. And when I felt anger toward people who couldn't let go of the past, I had to ask myself a hard question: Do they see me the same way?

I want to take this moment to personally apologize to anyone I have ever hurt over the years of high school and college. I may know I've caused some pain, and there may be others I'm unaware of. If you're reading this and feel any hurt or anger because of something I did, I hope you can find it in your heart to forgive me. Your feelings matter, and I truly regret any negativity I may have contributed to your life. Thank you for considering my apology.

Healing is a gift we give ourselves—and the generations that come after us.

Consider Jesus. He knew Judas would betray Him, yet He still welcomed him into the circle of His twelve disciples. He knew Peter would deny Him, yet He loved him unconditionally. Even when He looked upon a world corrupted by sin, He still chose to create, to love, and to redeem. And while suffering on the cross—mocked, beaten, and abandoned—Jesus responded with compassion. He forgave us and pleaded with the Father to show us mercy.

His actions reveal the true power of healing, forgiveness, and unconditional love.

For a long time, I believed Jesus didn't experience emotions the way we do. But Scripture paints a vivid picture of His humanity. He felt betrayal, hurt, sadness, anger, disappointment, and even fear. There was a moment when His fear was so intense that His sweat became like drops of blood (Luke 22: 39-46). That image stays with me. I can't imagine a fear so overwhelming that it manifests physically like that. Despite Him having fear He was still obedient.

None of us could ever replicate the sacrifice He made—dying a brutal death on the cross. He willingly laid down His life, offering us the precious gift of salvation. Even when I find myself in chaos, expecting Him to swoop in and fix my mess, He still forgives me.

And that realization changed everything.

## A Lesson on the Trail

Let me share a humorous and eye-opening story that helped me understand this truth more deeply.

My mother-in-law was visiting for her birthday, and we decided to go hiking. We're all outdoor lovers—even my oldest son was excited to run along the path. At the time, I had no clue I was pregnant with baby Noah. But what started as a fun adventure quickly turned into a struggle. The trail felt endless. My feet throbbed. My knee protested with every step. Cramps seized my foot. Tears threatened to fall.

Meanwhile, my mother-in-law kept cheerfully reminding us, "If the Lord brought us to it, He will help us through it."

Finally, I snapped. I threw my hands up and yelled, "Jesus, get me out of here!" Then I turned to her and said, "Jesus didn't bring us to this trail—we chose this path ourselves, and now we're expecting Him to rescue us from it!"

**And yet... He did.**

**He always does.**

Sometimes we walk ourselves into situations and still expect divine intervention—and God, in His mercy, shows up anyway.

## Choosing Forgiveness

If I can experience that kind of forgiveness, then nothing can prevent me from offering forgiveness to others. I'm not saying it's easy; I'm human, and my feelings do get hurt. However, I choose to forgive—sometimes even before the hurt occurs. Being hurt is part of the human experience, but what we can control is how we respond.

Forgiveness is not for the other person.

Forgiveness is for you—and for the generations that will follow.

As a mother, I think about my boys future. I want them, their children, and their children's children to know a version of me that is healed, whole, and emotionally free. That means I must start with myself.

I must forgive myself for:

- not extending grace when it was needed
- speaking negatively about myself
- letting others' opinions shape my worth
- acting out of pain and hurting others
- striving for perfection that was never required

And I also had to forgive myself for being angry at God.

Yes, God.

I had to acknowledge the anger I held toward Him—the disappointment, the resentment, the belief that He had abandoned me. I had to apologize for placing Him in a box, limiting His power based on my expectations. Many of us don't realize we're angry with God, but that hidden anger becomes a barrier in our spiritual lives.

### Healing for the Next Generation

I never want my sons to miss out on moments with me because I was too afraid to be vulnerable. I never want to look back and regret not pursuing my dreams because I let insecurity win. I refuse to let the voices of doubt from my past dictate my future.

Forgiveness frees me.

Forgiveness strengthens me.

Forgiveness aligns me with the grace Jesus freely gives.

How can I claim to know the depth of His grace and not extend that same grace to others?

I want to create a legacy of resilience and compassion for my boys—that's the future I want for us.

Releasing that anger opened a door I didn't know was closed.

By forgiving myself, and forgiving others, I'm cultivating a healthier, more fulfilling life—not just for me, but for everyone who comes after me

### A Word for You, My Friend

I may not know what you've been through. I may not know who hurt you or what challenges you've endured. But hear me clearly:

You should never have had to experience that, and it was not okay.

You don't have to forgive anyone today, but I encourage you to start with forgiving yourself today. Start with loving yourself and treating yourself with kindness. Once you make that choice, the rest will follow.

Know that I see you.

And even if I'm not physically with you as you reflect on these questions, the Lord is sitting right beside you. I felt His presence every time I wrote these words.

Heal, my friend—not for others, but so you can one day see the Lord face-to-face with His arms open wide. Allow yourself to cry. Allow yourself to feel. But remember to heal and forgive.

## Journal Reflection Prompt

*How has Christ forgiven you?*

*Who do you need to forgive right now?*

*Why is forgiveness necessary for your healing?*

_____
_____
_____
_____

*Forgiveness is not just about the person you're forgiving; it's about your own healing and growth. It allows you to release burdens that may be weighing you down and clears the path for a more positive and fulfilling life.*

*To start the process of forgiveness, you can take a few steps:*

*1. Acknowledge the Hurt: Recognize what has happened and how it has affected you. Write it down if it helps.*

*2. Decide to Forgive: Make a conscious choice to let go. Remind yourself that forgiveness is often more for your peace than for the other person.*

*3. Communicate:* **If it feels right**, *you might consider having a conversation with the person to express your feelings and your desire to forgive.*

*4. Let Go, Not forget: Release any lingering resentment. This may take time, but every step you take will bring you closer to healing.*

*5. Forgive Yourself: Remember that holding onto guilt or anger against yourself is as damaging as holding it against others. Understand that everyone makes mistakes and work on loving yourself through them.*

*Forgiveness can be a journey, but with each step, you move closer to peace and fulfillment.*

## Chapter 7: SURPRISE!

### *1 Peter 2:9 (NIV)*

*But you are a chosen people, a royal priesthood, a holy nation, God's special possession, that you may declare the praise of him who called you out of darkness into his wonderful light.*

As I reflect on my childhood traumas and the lasting impact they've had on my life, I find myself standing at a meaningful crossroads. After writing this book, praying through my emotions, and working consistently in therapy, I've come to understand something I never expected: the challenges I faced were necessary for my growth. It may sound strange, but I truly believe I needed to walk through those struggles—being bullied, feeling unsupported, and navigating a system that didn't see me—because they shaped the purpose God has called me to fulfill.

Revisiting those memories was overwhelming at first. I feared it would break me all over again. But instead, this journey revealed the strongholds that had controlled me for so long. Now I can see how those obstacles fueled my desire for change—not just for myself, but for the generations that will come after me.

Without those hardships, I might never have found the strength to persist. I might never have written this book. I might never have pursued my Doctorate in Education with a focus on disabilities and the broken policies that often harm more than they help. Had I not taken the time to reflect, I would likely still be holding onto anger toward the school system instead of working within it to amplify the voices of students with hidden learning disabilities and the faculty who struggle to support them.

This journey has taught me compassion, resilience, and the importance of advocating for change—both in our communities and within ourselves.

## Pain and Purpose Are Often Connected

Our journeys are often intertwined with pain and purpose, both flowing from the same well of experience. When we lay our struggles before the Lord with complete surrender, He transforms our pain into something meaningful. Just as Jesus endured unimaginable suffering in silence, we can find strength in quiet resilience, trusting that our Heavenly Father fights alongside us.

While the weight of the cross He carried is beyond our comprehension, we all carry our own burdens. We must pick up our crosses and confront our challenges. As we navigate healing, we begin to see how the Lord walks with us—shoulder to shoulder—bearing our struggles. If you ever feel isolated in your pain, know this: **you are not alone.**


## Creating Your Own Surprises

Let's embrace a proactive mindset. We are not here just to take up space on this earth. Each of us has a meaningful purpose in the kingdom. Our journey should be filled with joy, even in the midst of uncertainty. We can transform our pain into purpose and begin creating our own moments of surprise.

These surprises aren't about impressing others or seeking validation. They're about stepping boldly into the plans God has for us.

For me, one of those surprises has been letting go of the belief that I'm not good enough, smart enough, or worthy enough. I've taken courageous steps—pursuing my doctorate, writing this book, and choosing healing daily. I don't know what lies ahead. I don't know where my degree will take me, how many people will read this book, or whether I'll write another one.

But I do know this:

I will continue to choose healing.

I will continue to use my waiting seasons wisely.

### Waiting Seasons Are Not Wasted Seasons

When I talk about waiting seasons, I mean those times when everything feels overwhelming, and hope seems distant.

Despite all the chaos, I choose not to worry or try to control everything. Instead, I spend time daily with the Lord, surrendering my will and my plans. I pray, "Your will, not mine. Your plans, not mine. Lead me, Lord. Take the wheel."

My life may look different from what others expected for me—or even what I expected for myself—but that's okay. This is the journey the Lord sees for me. And I invite you to embrace the same truth.

God has incredible plans for you.

You are not forgotten.

He wants you to come to Him and lay your burdens at His feet.

Even Jesus experienced fear before the crucifixion. He prayed in the garden, asking if there was another way. In that moment of vulnerability, the Father sent an angel to comfort Him (Mark 14: 32-42). If Jesus faced fear and uncertainty, then it's okay for us to feel the same. Our Heavenly Father will always comfort us when we come to Him with honesty and boldness.

You are not alone in this journey. We are walking toward a brighter future together—with faith, hope, and courage.

### A Word to You, My Friend

I know revisiting your toughest challenges isn't easy. I'm grateful you walked through this journey with me—not as an observer, but as someone willing to reflect, feel, and grow.

Thank you for your courage.

Thank you for your strength.

Thank you for recognizing that the Father has been with you every step of the way.

I'm proud of you, my friend. I wish I could give you a warm hug right now.

Keep journaling.

Keep asking the hard questions.

If you haven't started yet, grab your favorite pen, anoint your hands, and begin breaking free from the chains that have held you back from His grace, love, and mercy.

And if you're wondering why you're reading this, or what the purpose of this message is, I want you to know something clearly:

**I love you.**

I'm sending blessings to you, your family, and the generations that will come after you—those you may never meet, but who will benefit from the healing you choose today.

*Until next time…*

## Journal Reflection Prompt

*How does it make you feel knowing that Jesus faced every emotion we encounter?*

*Does this truth make it easier to go to Him in prayer?*

*Understanding that Jesus faced every emotion we encounter daily can significantly shift our perception of Him. It makes Him more relatable and accessible, showing that He truly understands our struggles. When we experience joy, sorrow, anger, or doubt, we can find comfort in knowing that He has walked a similar path. This connection can deepen our empathy and compassion for others, as we recognize that everyone has their own battles. It also encourages us to express our feelings more openly, knowing that they are a part of the human experience and that Jesus embraced them fully.*

## Who Jesus Says You Are: A Friendly 7-Day Identity Devotional

Sometimes the hardest part of healing is remembering who you truly are. Not who people said you were. Not who your past tried to shape you into. Not who shame whispered you'd always be.

This section is here to remind you — gently, simply, and clearly — of who **_Jesus_** says you are.

Take your time with each one. Let the truth settle in. Let it speak to the places that still feel tender.

## How to Use This Devotional Section

Before you begin these 7 days of discovering who Jesus says you are, I want to invite you into something a little different — something that helps the truth settle deeper.

Each day includes:

- A short devotional

- A simple prayer

- A journal page

- **And one more thing:** a Scripture with a missing word for you to look up and fill in

Why?

Because there's something powerful about opening your Bible for yourself. When your eyes land on the words, when you fill in the blank with your own hand, the truth becomes personal. It becomes yours.

**How It Works**

1. Read the devotional for the day.

2. Look up the Scripture reference in your Bible.

3. Find the missing word or phrase.

4. Write it on the blank line provided.

5. Sit with it. Let it speak to you.

6. Use the journal page to reflect on what God is showing you.

This isn't about getting the "right answer."

It's about slowing down, listening, and letting God remind you who you truly are.

**Take your time.**

Let the Word meet you where you are.

And let each day draw you deeper into the identity Jesus has already spoken over your life.

## Day 1

**You have** _____ **and** _____

**Scripture:** Ephesians 1:7

### Devotional

Redemption means nothing in your past is wasted. Forgiveness means nothing in your past is held against you. Jesus rewrites your story with grace, not guilt.

### Prayer

Jesus, thank You for redeeming my life. Help me walk in the freedom of forgiveness every day.

### Journal Reflection Ideas

1. What part of your past still feels heavy…

2. How does God's forgiveness change the way you see yourself…

## Day 2

**You are a New _____**

**Scripture:** 2 Corinthians 5:17

**Devotional**

When Jesus makes you new, He doesn't patch up the old pieces — He transforms you from the inside out. Your past no longer has authority over your identity. Every day becomes an invitation to walk in the freedom He already secured for you.

**Prayer**

Jesus, thank You for making me new. Help me release the old stories I've carried and step fully into the life You've created for me.

**Journal Reflection Ideas**

1. What part of "new" feels hardest for you to believe today…

2. What old story or label are you ready to release…

## Day 3

**You are** _____

**Scripture:** 1 Peter 2:9

**Devotional**

Being chosen by God means you were wanted, seen, and intentionally set apart. Not because of perfection, but because of love. When the world overlooks you, God calls you His own.

**Prayer**

Lord, remind me daily that I am chosen by You. Let this truth silence every voice that says I am not enough.

**Journal Reflection Ideas**

When have you felt unseen or forgotten…

What might God be choosing you for in this season…

## Day 4

**You are God's** _____

**Scripture:** Ephesians 1:5 & Romans 8:17

### Devotional

You are not an outsider trying to earn a place at the table. You are a beloved child with full access to the Father's heart. Jesus didn't just save you — He adopted you.

### Prayer

Father, thank You for calling me Your child. Teach me to rest in Your love and trust Your care.

### Journal Reflection Ideas

What does being God's child mean to you personally…

Where do you still feel like you have to earn love…

## Day 5

**You are His** _____

**Scripture:** Ephesians 2:10

**Devotional**

You are God's intentional design — crafted with purpose, beauty, and meaning. Nothing about you is accidental. Every gift, every scar, every chapter is woven into His plan.

**Prayer**

God, help me see myself the way You see me — created with purpose and designed for good works.

**Journal Reflection Ideas**

What part of yourself is hardest for you to appreciate…

How might God want to use your story for good…

## Day 6

**You are called Out of** _____

**Scripture:** 1 Peter 2:9

**Devotional**

Jesus didn't just pull you out of darkness — He invited you into His marvelous light. Shame loses its grip when you step into the truth of who He is and who you are in Him.

**Prayer**

Lord, thank You for calling me into Your light. Help me walk boldly in the freedom You've given me.

**Journal Reflection Ideas**

What "darkness" have you been carrying or hiding…

How does God's light bring clarity or comfort…

## Day 7

**You are Part of a Holy** _____

**Scripture:** 1 Peter 2:9

**Devotional**

You belong to a people set apart by grace. Holiness isn't about perfection — it's about belonging. You are part of God's family, His kingdom, His story.

**Prayer**

God, thank You that I belong to You. Set my heart apart for Your purposes and Your glory

**Journal Reflection Ideas**

How has God shown that you belong…

What does living "set apart" look like for you…

**Dear Readers, Prayer:**

Oh Lord,

I come boldly to seek your forgiveness for my sins. I come repenting and surrendering my entire life to you, Father. I come to express my sorrow for any plans in my mind that are unlike yours. Lord, I ask that you remove anything from my life right now that prevents me from hearing from you, seeing you, and being filled with your Holy Spirit. Lord, let your Holy Spirit teach me everything I need to know and help me remember any details you have shown me.

Lord, thank You for the immense love You've shown me. It's through Your grace that I have experienced transformation, protection, and guidance in my life. I am grateful for Your presence in all the trials I face, knowing that I am never alone. Please help me build my life on a foundation of love anchored in You, ensuring that I stand strong and unwavering.

Remind me of Your love, especially in moments when I feel unworthy or unloved. Help me to release any torment that threatens this foundation, as I seek to cast out fear, which is not of You. Mend my heart, restoring the brokenness within me and reclaiming what has been lost. Clear away anything that obstructs my capacity to love fully and openly.

I ask for strength in my faith, Lord. Increase my belief in You, and let Your mercy flow into my heart, especially for those I may have ill feelings toward. Nothing is impossible for You; I long to move forward toward the future You have prepared for me. Guide me on this journey and help me to embrace the wonderful plans You have in store.

Lord, please renew my inner self and fortify my spirit so that I do not waver in challenging times. May the transformation within me shine through to the world around me. I am eager to press forward into all that is waiting for me, trusting in Your perfect timing and purpose.

In Jesus' mighty name,

**AMEN!**

I am justified by **faith**!

I have **peace** with God!

I have **access** because of my faith!

**Grace** for what is ahead of me!

Rejoice in what is ahead of me even if I do not have it **yet**!

Rejoice in my suffering because it will **produce** my patience!

**Hope does not disappoint us!**

## About the Author

Hi, I'm **Brianna Echavarria** — a wife, mom, scholar, and woman who has learned firsthand that God's grace shows up in the most unexpected places. I grew up in Newark, New Jersey, where I faced challenges that could have easily silenced me: hidden learning disabilities, bullying, and an education system that didn't always know what to do with a girl like me. For a long time, I believed the labels spoken over me. But God had other plans.

I'm someone who was told I would never read at grade level, never graduate on time, and never make it to college. Today, I hold a bachelor's degree, a master's degree, and I'm pursuing my Doctorate in Education. Not because the journey was easy — but because God kept carrying me through every season I thought would break me.

My passion is simple: I want people to feel seen. I want students with hidden learning disabilities to know they're not alone. I want mothers, daughters, and anyone who has ever felt "not enough" to know that God's grace is bigger than every limitation, every label, and every lie.

When I'm not writing or studying, you can find me laughing with my husband, Noel, and chasing after our sons, Nathan and Noah. I love journaling, worship music, and those quiet moments when God whispers something to my spirit that I didn't even know I needed.

This book is part of my testimony — not of perfection, but of perseverance. Not of having it all together, but of learning to surrender. If my story helps you feel understood, encouraged, or a little less alone, then every tear I shed writing these pages was worth it.

Thank you for walking through this journey with me. I pray my words remind you that grace is real, healing is possible, and your story is far from over.

Made in the USA
Coppell, TX
08 March 2026

73236398R00042